THIS KIND OF KNOWING

THIS KIND OF KNOWING

SUSANNAH SHEFFER

Cooper
Dillon

Acknowledgments:

Grateful acknowledgment is made to the editors and staff of the
following publications, in which some of these poems first appeared:

Bear River Review: "Deciding," "How My Father Named Me,"
    "Tracks," "Doubt," "A Knowledge Like Glass,"
    "The Silence," "Like This," "Last Visit"

Poets On: "In Boston"

Sing! Heavenly Muse: "Art Class"

This Kind of Knowing
Copyright © 2013 by Susannah Sheffer
First edition

Cooper Dillon Books
San Diego, California
CooperDillon.com

Cover Art & Design: Max Xiantu

ISBN-10: 0-9841928-7-5
ISBN-13: 978-0-9841928-7-8

Printed in the United States

TABLE OF CONTENTS

To the memory of my father
Isaiah Sheffer
1935—2012

CAVING

Take the fear
and bring it with you
as you enter
the chill opening
that accepts but does not
welcome you.
Make yourself
still and tight as memory
as you crawl on your belly
through the jagged passage.
And even if
you can't lift your head
and panic rises inside you,
keep going. Feel the mud
make a canvas of your clothes,
turning them into the crusted skin
of someone you've never been until now.
Maybe you will come out of this
glorious, but for now
shine the flashlight so you see
what you can.
At last, stand up
in the inner chamber
and feel the radiance of every muscle.
Place your hand
flat against the rock
and feel the beads of water there
like something blooming,
like something you never imagined
but realize with surprise
that you could, actually, love.

DECIDING

Summer evenings when the opera singer
practiced and practiced her aria
I lay at the window listening

until the notes sounded like they came
not from any one body
but from the world itself

doing what it had to do: splitting open
into lament, the vowels
that would go on and on

if no one stopped them. By themselves
they would never resolve
into form; they would stay

in the open mouth,
the melody that cannot help itself,
scaling and continuous.

So what I had to do, lying there
on the bed, humid with wanting
and not wanting to listen, was

hold out my hands and
make myself into the shape
that something needs

in order to be
caught and cradled,
able to bear being told.

HOW MY FATHER NAMED ME

Because I came too early,
because I had had enough and wanted more,
they weren't ready, they were caught,
they would have held me back,
said *give us a little more time.*
This was not how they'd pictured it,
but then who's to say they pictured anything,
who's to say they understood the longings
this third person would satisfy, or create.
So he left the hospital to stand in the park,
stepping out of the scene
in order to see it more clearly.
He thought it might come to him there
the way things sometimes come
if we stand in the right place,
hold ourselves the right way.
He thought he might learn to recognize
what he had been given,
what had burst into his life,
breathing and actual,
not an idea but something that had entered
in its own way and own time,
something that needed a name.

TRACKS

I have run my fingers over them:
Braille for the curious, the foolish, the brave.
I have flung myself at the door of a world
I might as easily choose
not to enter. But sometimes we want
proof: sometimes this kind of
knowing, this abject demonstration
of what was done, and to whom.
The body is its own relief map,
marking the contours of exile,
or loneliness.

        So how to come back?
You returned to the old neighborhood,
slice of the handcuffs
still marking your wrists. But it was all right
because there at the table were
people who loved you, people who took you in
to the space they'd kept open,
pot bubbling on the stove, meals and meals
they had waited to serve you.
The scars on your arms faded only
slowly. Why was this what I wanted
to study? Everyone was looking elsewhere.
It's a curious thirst, a dangerous comfort,
my fingers skimming the pulse of the earth
to seek its unruly evidence.

WITNESS

I saw you taste it. I saw
when the ocean broke open
and you knew, like salt in the mouth:
this failure was yours.
Your job was to save his life
and you didn't do it.
What is it like? Tell me.
You put your hand to your chest
to show me: this is where I carry it.
The heart is not always the place to turn
for reassurance. In that gesture,
an agony of knowing, stones
at the bottom of the sea.
And then what? What happened next?
The last visit. You had to tell him
you couldn't stop it.
In a few minutes the guards would come for him.
What does it mean that even now,
the stench of confinement
or sudden news or certain scenes
in the movies can make you feel
as if *you* are dying? What does it mean that
if you sleep at all you still dream of dread?
So much happens that no one sees. I saw this.
And sometimes now in my own mind
I make the motions of swimming,
to try to feel for myself the rise and swell,
the promise and peril, the impossible comfort,
the salt we sometimes allow each other to taste.

OFF SEASON

Watch how far I will go:
down to the end
of this frozen peninsula,
with the sand spattering like hail
against the windshield,
into the chill embrace
of this unwelcoming season.
When we arrive,
the beach is so windy only a fool
would walk it. I am
that kind of fool.
                    I am willing
to see it, everything you dare to show,
every spare, winter-lit underside. I will be
more than a tourist with you.

The houses bone-still against the sky,
signs on the storefronts saying
closed till next year. I break a twig
from a tree, like breaking a strand
from a web; it's completely iced over
as though dipped in glass.
I am, irrefutably, here
for whatever comes next, for
whatever strange beauty I can discern.
At the end of the day
I look down at the twig
and—see what I've done?—
I've burned a fingerprint into it.

COURAGE

What can we make of the body?
We can make devotion,
the way Annie did,
sitting every day at Helen's side,
spelling the professors' lectures
into the soft dome of her hands.
Yes I see this is praiseworthy,
I see that history remembers
the way a body sits next to another
and gives itself over,
hour after hour, word after word.
But think of Helen,
the way she had to enter trust
so fully, step into it each day
and inhabit it, opening her hands
to the woman she loved. She made herself
an open thing, a receiving thing,
she knew this was
the real courage—turning herself, palms up,
to the story the world had to tell.

WHAT WE NEED

Without serpent, without temptation,
without the leathered underside of
desire, there would be nothing to tell about
or to mourn. Would that be better?
No stain of regret? Wouldn't you miss
the snake and his cunning, his way of
showing you all of yourself?
And how you are always, now, remembering
that eager taste, that offering, how
you saw it and wanted it—
bite, burst, feast in the mouth—
and how you imagined you could have
that swallow and still be,
somehow, wholly loved?

LIKE THIS

I want to be the one who
keens inside you, whose mourning

tangles itself with yours—seaweed mesh
of the heart—so you have to look again

to see which is mine. I should be wanting
distinctions, the clarity of two people,

but instead this briny confusion, so that
I might think I don't know what I mean.

But the tangle *is* the sculpture. There might
be a way to be clearer, to sort out the bodies

and feel only one. But no. I want to be known
not like that but like this.

DOUBT

What would it take to know for sure?
Knowing enters the body and then it hides.
You have to find it again. By the feel of
the shoulder blades, by the rise in the throat, the gut.
Knowing doesn't strip itself down
and show you. It's not a blueprint.
It's more like the corner of your bedroom,
the smell of fingerprints on a wall. It's like
crouching in the rocks above a familiar park
and a small boy asking *are you lost?*
You're not. It would be easier
if you were. You're standing apart from yourself
and looking down. The bones in your wrist
are loose and rattling and you imagine the cure
would hurt worse than the breaking. But maybe not.
You couldn't paint the color of fire
but you know what it is.
Maybe there is a way to present your bones for repair.
Maybe there is a place you can go.
These carousel horses aren't real
but each time you come around,
someone is there looking back at you.

WHAT HAPPENS

In the cage where the heart paces,
counts out the seconds, waits
for someone outside
to imagine its hungers.
Captive, it sharpens the
hard edge of need,
scraping against available
surfaces. Held,
as the Japanese say, in this
woven basket of bones,
the heart works to comfort itself,
or to take measure
of what is stored there.

HANSEL

As far as she knows,
I am only bone.
I refuse to show
how fat with hunger I really am.
Swollen with fear, ripe
with everything I have
taken from her,
I stick the deceiving bone
through the bars
and she cries out that I am
so lean and stubborn
I must not be human.
Inside my cage, I am too human
to contain myself—so doomed, voracious,
and far from home.

A KNOWLEDGE LIKE GLASS

Afterward you reach for it
like a marble in the pocket,
a private certainty
that only your hand knows.
This is what you hold,
what you tell yourself,
what people cannot tell
by looking at you,
what the moon would be
if you took it into your mouth
and sucked it smooth,
what the fire has cooled and become.

FUNERALS

Everyone said *flush them away*
but we wouldn't hear of it—
better to have cardboard caskets
inlaid with cotton, our own music
and a carefully worded goldfish eulogy.
Better to crouch together
beside a knotted tree, city twilight
dusting the sky.

                  Did you think of this
later, faced with an impossible burial,
the sky now a steely band of despair?
Did you realize then how little you knew?
Or could you remember your old rules
for even the smallest loss:
draw a precise ceremony around it,
cover it with dirt and blossom, and mourn.

THE SILENCE

You've swallowed the moon.
It swells inside you
until you are gravid with refusal to talk
or to leave the desperate company
of others. *Is something
wrong? Why are you so quiet?*
You don't tell what you've done.
Finally the poison works
in ways no one can miss:
the trembling legs, convulsive
not like sobbing but like protest
or surrender.

After they take you away,
the sky is a taut, blank canvas,
without trace of the radiant disc,
the luminous story
you took with you and did not yield.

BUILDING THE GRIEF HOUSE

It's my birthday
and you're drunk
and crying.
As you pull me up
to dance, ignoring
the other guests,
you plead
tell me how to do this.

All right, you're learning.
You're learning
how to build a house.
You carve out the rooms.
The walls swell until they
take the shape of your life.
You will open a window,
you will set things on the table,
you will choose furniture.
Who will live in this grief house
with you? The boy you were
will be there, drinking orange juice,
watching the raindrops cling
to the rooftops outside, waiting
for the doorbell to ring.
The woman you are mourning,
the one who gave you
what you love,
will crouch on the mantle,
a strange and watchful bird,
and you will have her wings,
they will beat inside you like her music.

You will wake each morning,
rosin the bow, tune the strings.
There are apples on the table,
bruised by the sun,
and this is the house you live in.

FLYING AGAIN

Go ahead, leave the earth
to its own devices.
Let all the fury and noise of it
go on without you.
You've been bound to it for so long,
without flight, without view,
just nights at the bedside,
awake to her pain.
Inside those long hours,
sleeping would have been
like flying: it would mean
leaving the vigil behind,
ignoring your own gravity.
But up here tonight, the earth
could be anyone, any blaze of lights
you're not responsible for.
Night will cede to day, again and again,
with you or without you. So fly over the houses,
the bridges, the cars chairs elevators train tracks
and every other magnificent thing
that isn't grief and isn't yours.

IN BOSTON

Here in your city
in a café called *Il Dolce Momento*
I order rich cocoa
for its stubborn sweetness
on the tongue, for the way it defies grief
so boldly. I sit with a stack
of your papers, caring about
exactly the things
that will save me: the commas,
the margins, the checking
of facts. Outside, the skaters
circle the ice with careful passion,
with instinct sharp as their blades.
The cellist who played at your bedside for days
has gone to a warmer city.
I am thinking of him
on the last morning of your life,
imagining that he played a few more notes
before getting up to tell everyone,
just because he was a cellist,
because that was what he knew how to do.
And so I'm doing what I know how to do.
We are what we are left with
so I am this sweet moment
and the way I wrap my hands around it,
refusing to be distracted
from my own survival.

FEEDING THE ANGEL

Day breaks over the city, spilling a thin light
onto the stones. In a few hours
the men will hose down this square,
but here, now, a moment of reverence
for bread, marmalade, sweet butter and *café au lait*
as the farmers pile green upon green
and fill barrels with olives
shiny as pebbles tossed
from sea to sand.

      This is what he wants: the details
of my life, slipped into his hands
like a secret deal we make over and over again.
How many times have I said *I don't want to?*
How many times have I tried to be
busy with other things? But mine is a demanding angel.
Here—I give him something to quiet him:
our last meal together, holding hands around the table
with friends. He said *I feel a pulse
but can't tell whose it is,* the hosts served warm bread,
raw peas, the children left the table to chase fireflies
on the grass, begged *catch me* as they dove into handstands,
slapping their cool ankles against our palms.

      Is this enough? No, he wants
more than memory. He wants what he can't have now:
those children grown up, their long hair reaching almost
to their narrow waists, and my own table in this foreign city
with the woman across the square laying out her strawberries

the way the earth laid them out for her, saying *take it*,
take every wild, sweet thing,
because you want it and I have made it
and this is what I am offering.

LAST VISIT

for Eve Merriam

In the poet's apartment,
the rooms rise over the city
like kites or balloons.
She sends me to get the phone.
I make her excuses.
The dying don't have to do
what they don't want to do.
Hers were the first poems I wanted
to crawl inside—like starfish,
a tangle of limbs becoming art.
Now we sit eating cake, her last offering
to pleasure—which, like
stubborn gravity, binds us here,
and which is, like her poems,
another form of praise.

THE MAKING

Think how the clay feels
when it gives itself to the sculptor,

when it yields to the hands, rises
to meet them
in a swell of surrender

so it can be returned to itself
as itself—

There, say the hands
as they deliver the bowl,
rounded and smoothed, the way
the sun delivers the earth to itself
each morning,
now you see what you are.

ART CLASS

Never fall in love with a line
said the art teacher
as we sat poised to fall in love
with anything, staring at her
taut and ready in our adolescent skins.
She ran her eraser across the easel,
showing us how not
to love: indiscriminately, stupidly,
wedding ourselves to what
no longer belonged.
Don't love it just because
it's easy, or beautiful,
or because you made it,
she said, her eyes like coal
in the center of her face.

*You think as long as you
have chosen something
you should keep it*, she told us,
her arms sweeping the paper,
fingers blue from chalk dust.
I wanted to hold that chalk,
let its texture seep into my fist,
and feel the world beating outside of me,
luminous, hard, not something I had made
or thought of. I would give up
what appeared beautiful, what I was proud of,
if I could have it, the whole drawing,
burning into me like real life.

IN THE STUDIO

I am the nude, sometimes blue,
sometimes dusty rose as though petals
had been rubbed into my skin.
I am a series
of poses. I am what he uses
to understand the world.
The smell of paint
is headier than any pine forest.
While I am keeping the pose
I whisper to myself the names of the colors:
Viridian. Ochre. Cobalt blue.

Now that he is old his hands are weak.
Painting has become too precise, too delicate;
it demands too much. But still he wants
to understand, so he uses
scissors, like a child. He cuts out large shapes
of women. He is still learning. The edges
tend to be rough. I watch him.
I listen to the scissors
scraping through the paper
like the blades of skaters on the ice.

He doesn't know
he has taught me to love the world
as much as he does. He thinks I cannot
see myself as I pose,
but he is not the only one with eyes.
I stretch the skin across my hips
like a canvas, I turn
so that my shoulder blades
become wings.

COMING BACK

(After reading Touching the Rock: An Experience
of Blindness, *by John M. Hull)*

At first it seemed only
a catalog of losses.
The sky, that great ceiling, dome
of limit and possibility: gone.
The faces, those collections
of hill and valley, light and shadow,
that would make delight fill my throat
like berries: also gone.
I walked, the streets now strange
and difficult, counting and counting
what I no longer had: a miser of grief.

But things began to return.
The sky came back
through the wind in the trees,
the faces rose like relief maps
under my fingers,
and the streets grew familiar
as I learned that presence meant *building*
and sudden absence meant *curb*.

The moon, of course,
was gone forever,
but I found it again
in the smooth stone in my palm,
as luxurious and exact
as an egg, and in the melting of a candy drop,
the sweet softness and then the solid core.

When I wanted winter
I would reach down
to the leather of my boots
where I knew a ring of white still bloomed
and bring my finger to my lips
for the faint taste of salt.
I found the winter tree
in the fine bones of my hand
and this was how
I took each discovery—

like the feeling of
running burlap through my teeth,
a texture welcome because it was so ungiving,
the odor musty, believable, saying
yes, this is a new door, but just the same it leads you
back to the world.

TRADING PRIMES

*J. would say a number ... M. would catch the number, nod, smile,
and seem to savor it. Then he, in turn, would say another number,
and now it was J. who received, and appreciated it richly.*
— *Oliver Sacks*

Call us men of the circus
if you need to, but understand
what kind of circus it is.

I toss one, lighter than a ball;
I can almost see the arc it makes
in the air. He catches it

and back and forth we go,
ascending higher and higher
to those reaches where

there are fewer to sustain us.
But each is luminous.
No one would ever call us

graceful, but for a moment
their grace is ours. We are
inviolable. We refuse

symmetry. But order
and a solid radiance: these
are what we know. I toss

another. He catches it
and savors its
holy, indivisible splendor.

RETURNING

Don't you remember?
You who have been a glassblower,
drawn that fiery silk across the air
as if you believed in it—

was it not always a miracle?

You who saw that distinct shape
everywhere, followed it where it led you,
did what it demanded that you do—

is there nothing there for you now?
Can you not believe that these lines
will make of your heart something
bearable, renewable,
something that keeps on beating
with dumb passionate insistence
no matter what the world does or doesn't offer it?

Can you not try?

You have been away from this place
for so long, this way of laying sticks
into the ground,
taking careful, undaunted steps
into the darkness,
cupping the potent, holy water
into your hands—

is there not something worth praising
in this posture, this willingness,
this taking and shaping,
letting the world make you thirsty
but then drinking,
holding something up and saying
ok, there is this.

What did you ever think it would do?
Is that more or less than what is happening right now?

So return to it, the way you return
to a lover's body,
knowing it is home and terrifying
all at once

because you will fail it repeatedly
and it will still deliver that
patient, unstoppable joy.

Susannah Sheffer is staff writer at the national organization Murder Victims' Families for Human Rights, and she also works with teenagers, helping them to understand their lives through writing. Her essays and poems have appeared in numerous magazines and journals, and she is the author of four books, most recently *Fighting for Their Lives: Inside the Experience of Capital Defense Attorneys* (Vanderbilt University Press, 2013). More information is on her website, SusannahSheffer.com.

www.ingramcontent.com/pod-product-compliance
Lightning Source LLC
Chambersburg PA
CBHW050429110726
47899CB00008B/2910